A Letter to Love

A book of poetry

A Letter to Love

A book of poetry

STEPHANIE LATRICE

Copyright © 2020 by Stephanie Latrice

All rights reserved. No part of this publication may reproduced, distributed, or transmitted in any form or by any means, including photocopying, recording, digital scanning, or other electronic or mechanical methods, without the prior written permission of the publisher, except in the case of brief quotations embodied in critical reviews and certain other noncommercial uses permitted by copyright law. For permission requests, please contact Stephanie Leflore.

Published 2020
Printed in the United States of America
ISBN: 978-1-7352534-1-1
Library of Congress Control Number: 2020911839

Cover Design by Teejay Spencer Creative Corp.
Back Cover & Interior Art by The BlaQ Knight
Edited by Elizabeth Ann Editing Services

Prepared for Publication by The Director of Creativity, LLC
For information, address:
The Director of Creativity, LLC
An EAR to Write Publishing, Co.
P. O. Box 31272
Knoxville, TN 37930

thedirectorofcreativity.com

Table of Contents

Acknowledgements 10
Introduction 13
Deep Sea Diving 15
Todo (Everything) 17
The Freedom of Your Love 19
Light After the Storm 21
Anesthetized 23
Leap of Faith 25
Dream Catcher 26
The Heart Grows Fonder 29
Rescue Me 31
Open Cave 33
Artistic Stroke 35
Rivers Cried 37
Why? 39
Eyes for You 41
Lay Up, Stay In 43
My Wind 45
Stop Pretending 47
Today is a Good Day 48
Because of Love 51
Ocean Paradise 53
Come Back to Me 55
War is Our Love 57
Seesaw 59
Head in the Clouds 61
Matters of the Heart 63
Dark Roads 65

Table of Contents, continued.

This is Me	67
April Fools	68
Summer Nights	71
Bare Face	73
Forgive Me that I Care	75
Evette	77
Tell Me Again	79
If I Make a Sound	81
When No One Else Will	83
Brown Amber	85
Forehead Kiss	87
I've Never Been in Love	89
Battered Heart Torn	91
The Window's Breeze	93
Love, is that you?	95
Steady Heartbeat	97
Broken Glass	99
Thunderstorm	101
Shadows Follow	103
Childhood Memories	104
Not Without You	107
"Hey Love"	109
Random Text	111
Heart on My Sleeve	115
Nothing You Could Do	116
Time is on Our Side	119
From Love to You	121
Balter	125
Black Ink	127
Tomorrow, the Sun Will Rise	129

It's Me Again	131
No Barriers	133
See Me	135
Hopeful Romantic	137
Maybe Not	139
About the Author	140

Acknowledgements

I first, always and forever, thank God who is my life and the giver of it. I thank Him for bringing me through all of my life experiences and relationships and giving me a voice to be able to share my thoughts in a poetic way that people can relate to and understand. I will continue to keep You first, and I pray this book helps others see love expressed uniquely, and that it carries someone through the good and bad of what they are facing.

To my family, I couldn't begin to explain how much your support means to me. Carrie and Stevie, I'm sorry I annoyed you when I wouldn't come out of my room some days. I hope you understand now that the words in my head and heart needed to come out. Thank you for your excitement, encouraging words, and love. It has pushed me to complete this book.

My wonderful friends and co-workers at Chicago Public Schools, Anthony, Jourdain, and Markus, I love all of you like family. You have shown me nothing short of support and encouragement. Thank you!

To those who have helped this vision come to life: To my good friends and awesome graphic designers TJ Spencer and Justin Walker, thank you for making the vision of the cover come to life. I am so grateful to have met such talented young black men who are incredibly willing and available to help me accomplish this. From the bottom of my heart you are greatly appreciated. To my newfound friend Elizabeth Antoinette, who has given me tips, and who has been a BIG help in guiding me through this process in editing and publishing my book, thank you so much!

Lastly, to Love. You have put an indent on my heart forever. You will always be the force behind every embrace, every passion, every kiss, every intimate moment, every time black ink hits white paper, and every time my fingers hit the keys on my keyboard. You bring out the corny, the weird laughs, the tears that stain my pillow, and my smiles.

Introduction

     I won't bore you with the semantics just because it's poetry. I hope the words in this book speak for themselves. I will tell you, however, to prepare for emotion to be brought out of you, because as each word written opens up deep feelings of passion, outlook, and sentiment within me, I know it would do the same for you. I hope each poem touches a part of your heart and soul that you never want to leave behind.

     I love the freedom that poetry gives and writing this has given me said freedom to be myself, to be creative, and not to be afraid to express my feelings. I want you to love this book and let it become a part of you in a profound and meaningful way.

Enjoy!

With love,

Stephanie Latrice

DEEP SEA DIVING

I want to dive below the surface,

no longer hiding behind the veil of fear and

oblivion.

I want to be entirely exposed to the

possibilities of what I can find.

I want you to break free beyond the exterior

of my mind and dominate me.

Why should I combat the inevitable fate of

being consumed in your love?

Your depths are endless, and my emptiness

needs to be filled.

So, consume me for what it's worth, and I'll

let the waters overtake me as I fall deep into

the aquatic abyss of your love.

TODO (EVERYTHING)

You are the fire within me.

No matter how ice-cold I want to be,

you melt me away.

You are the voice within me.

No matter how far I try to run from it, it whispers to

me, letting me know you are there.

You are a tornado within me.

I tried to plant myself in destruction, but wherever

you went, you pulled me in your path of love.

You are the life within me.

Erasing the towering rage of hurt and breathing into

my lungs, the strength to live again.

You are the melody to my muted song.

The harmony to my unstable, unhinged existence.

The polyphony to my incompatibility.

THE FREEDOM OF YOUR LOVE

I can't mask the smile that I tried so desperately to keep from breaking free.

The satisfaction I feel from you taking a chance on me, choosing me to be a part of your existence.

I can dance freely now.

The sun is smiling with me, delighting in my bliss.

No clouds, no gloom.

I breathe and the air is fresh.

No more toxic smells of hurt and disappointment.

My life is no longer heavy with the weight of depressive emotions of guilt and sorrow.

I long for you, even when you're next to me.

I cry for you, even while you wipe my tears.

I sit in the beautifully flowered field of your soul.

My fears are no longer a part of me but resting into outer darkness.

LIGHT AFTER THE STORM

After the storm has passed and the dew drops from the leaves…

After the tempestuous waves have calmed and the water has found her peace…

After the roaring wind ceased from his destruction…

You caress my cheek with the callousness of your hand.

You embrace me with the strength of your arms.

Your eyes are bright, full of assurance, and I'm dancing in the depths thereof.

ANESTHETIZED

Does it sometimes feel unreal?

The fact that I can love you for a lifetime and still never get tired of giving myself to you?

I always want more, I ever need more.

Is it possible to yet love in the depths of sleep?

Can my soul still yearn for you when my mind is unconscious to the world?

I want you to always know that even when I'm gone, my love will be happy it gave you a chance.

LEAP OF FAITH

You are my ocean and I'm standing on the shore. From here, you seem to go on forever. Unending. Are you as deep as you are far? Will I drown in the powerful waves that undulate without ceasing?

I hear you whisper as the water crashes on the sand. Your voice is still and quiet. The horizon painting you with colors of beauty and grace. For me to discover your depths, I have to leave the shore.

I'm unafraid.

DREAM CATCHER

You make me forget what it means to be afraid.

It's as if I've stepped over into another dimension that is surrounded by nothing but you.

No exit doors.

I'm trapped in your essence.

Not ever wanting to escape.

You make me forget what it feels to be abandoned and unwanted.

Yes, my heart has been wounded— the knife has cut deep into the tissue mass.

The blood had stopped flowing, turning my heart cold.

I died to love.

Oh, but to be revived!

New dawn peeking over the horizon.

The sun has kissed my skin again.

The warmth of its light filling my soul as if it never left.

Now, I know I'm here to stay…

In love with you.

THE HEART GROWS FONDER

There's something about pain that makes everything come into focus.

Since you left that's all I have experienced.

My mind can't rest, my heart can't sleep.

You brought back to life that part of me that I wanted to keep buried.

I only miss you when I'm breathing. You have consumed all of me.

You've challenged me in so many ways that I never thought could be possible.

You showed me how to feel again.

How to love...

RESCUE ME

My eyes are masked by the pain and sorrows of my surroundings.

My heart is scarred by those I thought were there for me.

I cry out for help, but no one hears me.

My voice is unheard of like a scream underwater.

I'm drowning, but I have no lifesavers.

All I want is to break free above the surface and breathe.

Can you resuscitate me?

Can you breathe new life into me?

OPEN CAVE

Flowing from my heart in the depths thereof,

an open cave that emanates so much.

Yet, no matter how much it gives, no matter the

magical mysteries it holds, no matter the treasures

that it keeps buried within, it can't keep away the

thieves, the curious, the ones who only eye the wealth

for themselves.

Where the treasure is, naturally so, my heart will be

there also.

And when I have received all that you've had to offer,

I'm left spent and deserted, hollow and void, unsound

and unbalanced, and soon, my cave will fall in itself.

ARTISTIC STROKE

You can be gentle, like the stroke of a paintbrush.

So precise, so clear-cut, so accurate. So determinate.

You can make a person feel as if nothing else matters, like being in a hypnotic state of ecstasy.

Those butterflies in my belly, they flutter from the fuel of you, their only source of existence, dominance.

Your preeminence so evident, it captures everyone in your path, pulling, like a moth to a flame.

The power in your voice that makes one release on command, cry from your words and hate you in an overthrow of passion.

RIVERS CRIED

Tonight, I cry for you.

The yearning stabbing me, asphyxiating me, 'till I can no longer think about anything but the memories of you.

The consciousness of my feelings is no longer substantive.

My eyes are an ocean of tears, and I'm drowning all over again.

"You need me," you say.

"I can take the pain away."

But my tears are my deposition of what you do to me, yet, being a declaration of truth, that I am deprived of you.

I broke my own heart loving you,

And yet, I am not whole without you.

WHY?

You are the sparkle of joy in my eyes,

You are the tears.

You are the swell of passion in my heart,

You are the anguish.

You are the force that no one can destroy.

Why can't I let you go?

Why is my soul a magnet to you?

I push you away yet pull you near.

My mind always remembers, and my heart will always long for you.

And all I want to know is, why?

EYES FOR YOU

You're all I can see.

I can't look for another to hold me.

I can't look for another to console me.

In oblivion, my feet walk towards you.

In desperation, my heart cries for you.

Even with my eyes blinded by tears,

Even with my wounds open for all to see,

It is you that holds the most excellent medicine that

even the best doctors can't dispense.

You are my cure.

You are the antidote to my damaged existence.

LAY UP, STAY IN

I am reminiscing the feel of your hands mindlessly running through my hair and how it gave my body tingles.

I can still feel the soft puff of your breath against my lips as you slept. A gentle reminder of your presence with me.

"Baby," you whispered.

You had to be dreaming, as your chest rose and fell slowly with each breath.

"I'm here," I responded.

Your lips pulled up into a faint smirk, which in turn I couldn't help but run my finger over them, a smile gracing my own lips.

This is love. Me, here with you.

This is love. You, here with me.

MY WIND

Gentle is the touch in which you embrace me,

and I welcome the soft caress of your touch.

The motion breeze is like a whisper, calming, and

soothing in my ear.

I deeply breathe in your air.

My lungs are dependent upon you.

I wish I could bottle up a piece of you, so I could

have a singular part of you that no one else has access

to.

STOP PRETENDING

When your atmosphere has been destroyed,

you can't come around as if nothing has happened.

Do you not see what you've done?

Do you not recognize the pain you've caused?

Stop making promises of a better future when you

can't fix what's happening now.

Stop pretending we're okay.

It's like taking two ends of something and trying to

bind them together without the piece in the middle.

What is the missing piece?

The missing piece is my heart.

TODAY IS A GOOD DAY

It seems I can breathe a bit easier.

Nothing is the same without you.

Your eyes lit up my world when it was weak and dull.

Your hugs made me feel worth belonging to you.

Your kisses made me feel happy you were mine.

But nothing can erase this pain I have now that you're gone.

Come back to me.

What would it take to see that smile?

What would it take to hear that sweet voice again?

I would rip my heart out and place it in heaven's arms if that meant you would be mine again.

It feels as if time is against me.

Some moments I feel I will be ok.

Other times I hear the sound of my tears filling my ears.

Maybe today isn't a good day for me.

Sometimes I don't feel it is possible to have one again.

But I will never give up hope.

BECAUSE OF LOVE

Why does the most painful hurt

come from the ones closest to us?

My heart feels as if there is a

pound of lead at the bottom.

The world, in my view,

is a constant blur through my tears.

Why does my body shut down when I think of you?

Why can't my mind let go of you?

OCEAN PARADISE

Last night I dreamt of you…

The sound of the ocean waves created such a calmness that I sighed in paradisiacal bliss…

Your laughter comes from a distance, and I instantly smile, pulling my shades up onto my head, only to see a figure running towards me across the sandy shore.

The sun shone around you so bright, leaving no room for darkness. Your presence made me forget about the cares of life. I had you again, and as I fell into your arms, I knew you would never let me go. You would hold on to me forever. Nothing could take this happiness from us. I kissed your neck, knowing that it was your ticklish spot. Your laughter sounded in my ear, and I could breathe again.

You lifted from my embrace, walking back towards the ocean. You picked up a hand full of sand and tossed it at me. I laughed, standing ready to sand battle with you. You laughed and began to run into the water.

"Bye," you said. You turned to wave goodbye, but I couldn't say goodbye yet. *"Wait! Let me come with you."*

But you were already gone.

COME BACK TO ME

I never realized how death could bring so much pain

until pain stood at the doorstep of my heart.

My memories play back in my mind like an old reel

film, and I'm there.

Watching the happy times, wishing I can pull them

out of my head and bring them back into reality.

Death may have taken you

but remembering is killing me.

I remember the smiles and my heart feels heavy.

When life was no longer in your body, the tears fell

from my face as I kissed your hand, still feeling the

warmth of the blood that was slowly turning cold.

All I want is for you to come back to me, to bring

that smile back to my face.

WAR IS OUR LOVE

There is no love without war.

A battle of the minds. A battle of hearts.

It could last for years.

The effects may last a lifetime and could drive us apart.

War.

Love.

We war in our love.

War is our love.

There is no war without our love.

A battle of our bodies until we are both left spent.

One will win, the other will lament.

We kiss each other's pain with such passion.

We caress having to let go with fervent heat.

Our minds are filled with war.

But our hearts are filled with love.

SEESAW

Why do you hate me when I try to give you my best?

Why do you make me cry even when my head is on your chest?

I would cross oceans for you,

so why don't you man-up to the test?

My heart feels for you,

while yours feels less.

Make me believe it's not true.

Don't be oblivious to the tears I pour out for you.

Numb the doubt away like how my body knows you can do.

And when I say, "I love you,"

Don't forget to say, "I love you, too."

HEAD IN THE CLOUDS

I didn't want to love before you loved me.

I didn't want my heart to feel before you even had feelings for me.

I thought I could stop myself from loving you.

But you were a force to be reckoned with.

I'm high in the sky.

In the clouds of your love.

MATTERS OF THE HEART

Your heart swells when it's in love.

You know, the fast beats

that make you lose your breath.

The flush of your skin

that it's almost too hot to touch.

Your mind becomes paralyzed,

Your eyes become blind.

And now your heart is in danger.

But danger and I have become affiliated because we

both want the same thing.

You.

My heart offers itself to you

because it's too much for me to have alone.

To become one with love

is all that ever mattered to it anyway.

DARK ROADS

Sometimes I feel I walk these trails alone.

Whatever's within is untold.

Along these dark roads, the trees talk to me and the wind flows.

The pavement carries my feet as they strode,

Along these dark roads.

My eyes feel pressured and the tears may explode,

But here I have solitude and the peace it holds,

Along these dark roads.

THIS IS ME

I'm happy as flowers that bloom in the spring.

Cheesing like a baby, all gums no teeth.

Yes, I'm corny like the bag next to the frozen peas.

I'm gentle like the river between the mountain's feet.

Softer than the petals on a summer rose.

Tougher than the nails on your Uncle's toes.

I'll love you till I can't remember to love myself.

I'll fight for mine until in me, there is nothing left.

No ponds, no lakes, but an ocean I'll cry.

No desserts, no cakes, but chicken I'll fry.

I'll make you laugh

till the world lights up with your smile.

I'll annoy you

to the point you don't talk to me for a while.

But at the end of the day you can't help it, you see?

You can't resist the fact that you know you love me.

APRIL FOOLS

My mind was so tired.

So overwhelmed of seeing you deteriorate right before my eyes, and yet I had to be strong for you. For me.

My love for you pushed pass how drained I felt in my body.

You meant more to me than I meant to myself, and I was ok with that.

It's been three years and there's still forever to go.

Yet you're in my mind so vividly and all I can think about is those last moments I had with you.

I wished it was a joke.

What a terrible joke that would have been…

But at least you'll still be with me.

I wished it was a game.

What a terrible game that would have been…

But at least my eyes will get to behold you again.

I wished somebody would have said, "April fools!"

But that day claimed you for itself

It's no longer a day of games

It's no longer a day to joke around

It is a day that I will forever remember

Because it became the day, I no longer had you,

the day my heart hit the ground.

SUMMER NIGHTS

Your passion carries like the thick heat on a summer night. The sunsets and the horizon paint a beautiful glow alight.

Your gaze from afar is as if the winter will never return, although it has the right.

But the depths in your eyes hold the fire of the sun until the fire in mine ignites.

The wind offers no relief, as my heated skin incites.

As you close the distance between us,

the sun behind you as your spotlight.

Your smile shoots a spark in my heart,

turning everything around us black and white.

Your hand travels to the nape of my neck, your grip firm, yet polite.

I sigh as your lips softly graze mine,

a promise of love on a summer night.

BARE FACE

I have flaws, some visible,

Some you can't see.

I have scars,

Most of them within.

I can't cover them, so I hope you'll still stay.

I'm not perfect, everything will be for you to see.

Do you mind the deformity?

The abnormality?

I want to open myself to you.

I want you to still love every blemish,

Kiss me without hesitation,

To protect my weakness.

So here goes nothing,

But everything.

FORGIVE ME THAT I CARE

I never gave you a reason not to care,

So, forgive me that I do.

I never gave you a reason to walk away,

But you still decided to.

I gave you my heart without hesitation,

So, forgive me that I still hold it out to you.

I never gave you a reason to not be faithful,

So, forgive me that I am.

Blood seeps from my soul,

the stains under your shoe.

I'm hurt to my core,

It's an empty shell in your hand.

Maybe tomorrow you will love me again

But I'm sorry, I still love you.

EVETTE

Her beam is brighter than the sun, her beauty better than that of the horizon

Her grin is so wide, you can't tell that she's numb

Sometimes her smile hides her pain

So bright, it blinds the truth inside

So, it takes a special someone to see past the shine

And when you see what's inside, you'll love her more than what is on the outside

Because inside she's imperfect

She's beautiful

Her flaws, flawless

Her hidden scars, a work of art

TELL ME AGAIN

Those words you say that turn the air dense like the

gravity in space

The way my fragrance smells when you brush your

nose against my neck

You love the way I grab the hair at the nape of my

neck when I'm nervous

I'm beautiful with tears

That you need me

Tell me you love me again

IF I MAKE A SOUND

I seem to have more pain than I do happiness

But if I make a sound, you may leave

You seem to ignore me more each day

But if I make a sound, you may tell me you don't

really care

Do you still see me?

If I make a sound, you may say I'm invisible to you

So, I best keep quiet, cause I don't want to lose you

But holding on to you is more damaging than actually

letting go

If I make a sound maybe, you'll hear me

A sound is better than the quiet words you give me

that leave me feeling empty

So, I'll sound the alarm, because it would be the only

thing to set me free

WHEN NO ONE ELSE WILL

God, only you see

You listen

You love

You protect

You save

You care

You forgive

When no one else will

BROWN AMBER

Swimming pools of brown amber eyes

A soft glowing speck brightens the irises of the soul

Brown like sugar

Warm like caramel glaze

Sweetly intense is the heat of your gaze

Brown amber hues

Stuck on me, until I get lost in you

I'm trapped in the depths and the possibilities

You see right through my body

to where my heart hides

With those brown amber eyes

FOREHEAD KISS

So delicate like the puff of a dandelion,

Yet it holds more meaning than any words

you've ever spoken.

My thoughts sometimes get the best of me.

I get anxious when you have to leave.

But the hushed touch of your lips somehow eases the

worry and simplifies the most complicated things.

I'VE NEVER BEEN IN LOVE

Love is in me

But I've never been in you

I've held you in my grip

But you always slipped through

Longing clothed me till I cried

You saw my teardrops fall

But you weren't ready to be the reason they dried

I've never been in you

But somehow you stayed in me so free

Until I realized I never really had you

It was just the yearning of wanting you to have me

BATTERED HEART TORN

I hate being in my thoughts

My heart tells me it needs love

My mind tells me I don't deserve it

I know what my heart needs

Sometimes I can't help but be torn between the two

THE WINDOW'S BREEZE

Your embrace surrounded me like a heavy blanket that I never wanted to leave.

Now the memory is a heavy burden I can't get rid of.

When I open my eyes, the emptiness next to me holds the unspoken truth.

My heart has a mind of its own,

it only wants to remember you.

Everything I see transforms into a version of you.

I try to sell my thoughts away hoping that that the wind carries them, but the breeze drifts back through my window at night.

And as I'm unconscious to the world, my eyes leak tears down my cheeks and your embrace surrounds me again.

LOVE, IS THAT YOU?

Is that you I see?

That blinding light from afar shining back at me.

Is it you I need?

You conquer the tempestuous waves, fighting for me.

Love, is that you?

My mind tells me I'm not ready, but my heart won't

let that stop me from loving you how I know I can.

And I hope nothing stops you from running through

any obstacle that tries to hinder your heart from me.

STEADY HEARTBEAT

Love still beats in my heart so steady

No matter the pain it has shown or given

I refuse to let love die within me

Love still beats in my heart so strong

I've cried a thousand times but smiled a thousand and one

So, love will forever pump blood through my veins

Until my heartbeats stop for the one who is ready to hold it in his hands

BROKEN GLASS

A glass shattered,

Like my heart did when you dropped it to the ground

It broke into tiny pieces

The glass is no longer whole

What was once perfect is now a beautiful mess

You remember my heart?

Yeah, the one you destroyed.

It can be transformed into the most beautiful artwork.

So, you see, I'm no longer your broken merchandise,

But I'm being made to be someone else's magnificent catastrophe.

THUNDERSTORM

I can't bring peace to your storm.

You can't cease the rain when I'm torn.

My lightning's flash strikes too soon.

Your thunderous roars shake the room.

It's until the sun peeks through, that I know I still have you.

SHADOWS FOLLOW

Sometimes I feel undeserving of love.

Maybe it's not written in the books for me.

I can't really explain why I feel this way.

Sometimes I feel I let God down too many times,

to the point, He may say no.

Or is it just the negative thoughts of my mind trying

to make me believe that I have experienced so much

pain in my life to never experience true love.

Too much pain has a way of shadowing the good

things until all is dark around me.

CHILDHOOD MEMORIES

Remember we used to play house?

Husband and wife with a crib full of kids?

You would pretend to leave, headed to work,

While I stayed home and cooked and cleaned?

Remember being on the block?

Block parties had people coming from around the way to play.

The smell of barbeque filled the air with old 90's jams.

The memory of being worry-free,

No broken hearts.

The memory of laughter and sharing candy.

No breakdowns or falling apart.

Childhood memories filled with jokes and fun,

Thoughts of being together forever, no falling in love.

Curfew hit when the streetlights shone at night.

Our mamas yelling at us to get inside, you could never tear us apart.

Those childhood memories that when you think of them now,

Makes you wish you could go back.

Those childhood memories that remind me of when I first gave you my heart.

NOT WITHOUT YOU

I am nothing without you

I can do nothing without you

I can't breathe without you

I can't live the next minute without you

You carry my soul in the palm of your hand

So, I can't even exist without you

I won't prosper without you

I can't even love without you

"HEY LOVE"

Can you help me wipe my tears?

I'm tired of doing it alone.

Will you defend me when I have to fight my fears?

I can no longer bear being tossed and thrown.

Will your arms wrap around me better than my covers at night?

Hey, Love,

People try to tell me how to feel, but when I feel, I write.

Hey, Love,

Your smile would lighten my dark world.

I need you to stay until the inner peace you give unfurls.

RANDOM TEXT
(A SHORT STORY POEM)

My phone buzzes and I take a chance to steal a glance. The moment I see "My forever" my heart does a dance. I look up to find there are no eyes on me, but at the board ahead. I look back down and open the message thread:

You asked me why I loved you yesterday, and I said that words couldn't explain. I didn't feel that was enough, and I wanted to give you an answer you deserve. A solution that comes from a place that only you own, and that's my heart.

The flutters in my heart drop down to my stomach, giving me butterflies. He did say words couldn't explain, and I was happy with that because I knew he meant it. A day never goes by without him showing his love to me, so I didn't question it. I begin to text back, "It's ok, babe," but another buzz interrupts, and a longer message appears:

Every time I look at you, all I want to do is implant my soul into yours and never leave. So, where my body can only go so far, my soul has already gone beyond me. So, it's not just why I love you, baby, but it's how much I want to love you more. I want to love you more than I already do. Harder than what you were used to before. Until my soul penetrates every part of your being. Until it's only me, you see, feel, and breathe. Your smile makes me want to continually find ways to keep it there. Your addictive laugh makes me want to always bury myself inside you until every broken piece is repaired.

I cover my mouth with my hand to hold in a sob. Tears roll down my face, you just made my heart throb. I've never read words so beautiful in my life, and they came from you. It only confirms more that I'm happy I said, "I do." I'm so blown away; I don't even know what to say next. So, I text back, "Babe, you just took my breath away. I'm speechless."

You deserve the world. I love you.

HEART ON MY SLEEVE

So vulnerable, yet I keep it exposed,

For all the world to see, but what's inside no one knows.

Don't pretend to see more than what's being shown.

You see, the stitches are there from the pieces I've sewn.

I let people get too close, they think my heart's a freestone.

But if I put it back in my chest, you won't be able to hear the intone.

So, I'll keep it on my sleeve, I will guard it, I'll be its chaperone.

It's tender, so precious like a stone.

I hope someone will hear my heart's voice,

So, I don't feel that I'm exposing it alone.

NOTHING YOU COULD DO

You couldn't stop her from loving you without measure.

Every ounce of her being seeped into you, though sometimes at a displeasure.

You couldn't cut the cords of her heartstrings, though you tried with much endeavor.

Her mind relentlessly fought through the anguish you gave; pain became her new possessor.

Yet, if you asked her how she felt, she would answer, "None the better."

There's nothing you could do to stop a strong woman, she's ever clever.

She knows one day you'll be back because you left her heart waiting, still holding on to forever.

And she's right back loving you as if nothing happened whatsoever.

You can't destroy someone gentle as a feather.

God will carry her through the wind, in His peaceful fair weather.

TIME IS ON OUR SIDE

Time flies,

But with you, it stands still.

The vast world moves on,

A blur all around us.

Time is nonexistent when I'm with you.

It stops for us so we could go on forever.

Its limited portal breaks so we can create our own universe.

It's you and me together.

Time is on our side.

FROM LOVE TO YOU

I'm watching you, but you don't know it.

It's so captivating how graceful you move.

I venerate in how hardworking you are, and how much love you have within you.

When you smile, the corners of my mouth instantly turn up. When you frown, my heart instantly wants to embrace you. I take pleasure in knowing you are mine alone and no one else's.

It's in the treasure that you hold, not just with your body, but the treasure that's inside your heart and mind. As you stand a ways off, I imagine different ways to express my love to you.

I would stand and walk over to you, and as you're washing the dishes, I would walk up behind you ever so gently, and slowly wrap my arms around you. My fingers would be splayed across your belly, and I would feel you relax into me.

I would then nestle my face into your neck as I begin to sway our bodies in a slow rhythm. I would inhale your scent and place a soft peck of love on your skin. I would brush my lips up to your ear and whisper my love for you that only you deserve to hear.

You have the propensity to affect me in such a way, I can't get enough of you. If I could use every word of emotion to express my gratitude to God for my blessing, it wouldn't be sufficient.

I give you everything that's in me, but I want to bestow more. At this very moment, my thoughts of you have me grinning from ear to ear.

You do that for me. Did you know that?

You somehow emanate exactly what I need from you without me ever having to say it verbally.

And when you read this, I hope you feel the very love floating off the paper into your soul.

Yours forever,

-Love

BALTER

Gracefully she dances.

Her moves are unrelated but perfect.

The music flows in her bones, carrying her away like a tornado across flat land.

She bends but never breaks,

she curves but never falters.

Her tears dance with her,

Her heart is a steady beating drum.

She bursts forward, only to stumble back with shame.

Her hands push out in front of her.

Her back arches in strength.

Her power is in her soul

as she fights against the wind.

She wins, undefeated,

Ending with you holding her heart.

And your heart she kisses forever within her.

BLACK INK

I think my pen may know me better than anyone.

It bears my deepest, darkest thoughts.

It stains the white paper,

writing my words with black ink.

It brings my thoughts to life,

Making every word come together when they fall

scrambled from my mind.

Sometimes I don't want to sleep,

lest I lose the feel of it in my hand.

When my emotions can't sleep, my pen writes for me

Filling that white paper with all that black ink.

TOMORROW, THE SUN WILL RISE

The throes of yesterday are no more divine.

But tomorrow a new horizon will shine.

The sorrows of yesterday have been

swept away with time.

A new joy is at the peak of a new day

when the sun will rise.

What is past are the pangs of hurt that made your

hand clutch your chest.

But it brings on the hope of a new day and lays all of

yesterday's pain to rest.

Yes, tomorrow is set in God's plan.

Yesterday we waved goodbye,

today we enjoyed the time.

For tomorrow, the sun will rise, and new dreams will

light our eyes.

Stephanie Latrice/*A Letter to Love*

IT'S ME AGAIN

Hello, it's me again.

We can pass the pleasantries.

I'm here with another bout of feelings you still haven't heard,

Another wound you still never tried to heal.

It's me. I'm here.

Don't look away because you might miss what's important again.

You can't sidestep what's right in front of you.

Hello? Can you hear me?

It's me again.

If you choose not to acknowledge me, just try not to ever forget me.

NO BARRIERS

The barriers of my heart,

I thought no one could destroy.

The walls were built from my wound's alloy,

Sealed with the fear of being a part of your decoy.

Somehow you broke past the grief,

to fill my heart with joy.

Your passion is the hammer to demolish the noise

that surrounds me;

The noise of the people that tell me I'm not good

enough to enjoy.

With you, there are no barriers,

As long as you're here they are null and void.

True love has no barriers.

Love makes itself impossible to avoid.

SEE ME

You see past the heavy rainfall.

Through the thick fog, I'm as clear as the day.

The night's darkness makes way for you.

There are no possibilities that you can't face.

There is no part of my heart that you haven't already seen,

When I try to hide deep within myself.

You show me life is not be faced alone,

And my fears are but forces that cause you to one day give up on yourself.

You never stopped seeing me,

I just need to learn to see myself.

You never stopped loving me,

It's just time for me to learn to love myself.

HOPEFUL ROMANTIC

The petals of a rose fade away into dust

Another grows anew

Your fingers touch the vibrant, delicate wings

Only to leave it to freeze over in the dew

Until another one grows anew

It hopes for your presence, in your absence it stings

But it will wait with patience

For you to come refresh, renewed

Then leave it wanting

Until another grows anew

MAYBE NOT

Will I get an apology from you?

Are you even sorry?

Should I continue to hold on to this?

Will things be different?

Would a new smile begin?

I love you, but will you finally show your love to me?

Maybe not, huh?

Hey, a girl could only dream.

About the Author

STEPHANIE LATRICE was born and raised on the southside of Chicago, IL. Being the middle of five children, [she always felt to have a special talent which is writing. She first discovered her passion for romance and writing in grammar school at the age of fourteen and learned how to use her emotions and thoughts to bring out beautiful words of poetry.

Stephanie's experience with love has been a rollercoaster of events that have shaped her into who she is today. Whether the experience was direct or indirect, it still left an impact on her life that opened her mind to different viewpoints on love. No matter the pain she has been dealt, she vows to hold on to love, for God indeed is love. Stephanie hopes to one day experience true love, as she continues to wait on the perfect timing of God to send that special one her way.

At the age of 28, Stephanie currently works for the third largest school district in the country, Chicago Public Schools. She has been with CPS for two years. She endeavors to write more books of poetry, with the goal to one day write her first novel. You can follow Stephanie on these social media platforms:

Instagram: @stephanie.latrice
Facebook: Stephanie KeepinGodfirst Leflore
Snapchat: stephiegirl22
YouTube: Women of Strength

www.ingramcontent.com/pod-product-compliance
Lightning Source LLC
Chambersburg PA
CBHW071701040426
42446CB00011B/1862